W9-BDK-488

GRAND
CANYON

GRAND CANYON

Text and photographs by Patrick Cone

Carolrhoda Books, Inc./Minneapolis

Thanks to: Judy and Peter Weiss, and the rest of the Grand Canyon river guides

Text and photographs copyright © 1994 by Patrick Cone, except where photograph credits are otherwise noted.
Series editor: Marybeth Lorbiecki

Additional photos and illustrations are reproduced through the courtesy of: National Park Service/Mike Quinn, pp. 22 (top, bottom), 23; The Museum of Fine Arts, Houston; Gift of Miss Ima Hogg, p. 26 (bottom); The Smithsonian Institution, National Anthropological Archives, Bureau of American Ethnology Collection, p. 27; National Park Service, p. 29; Denver Public Library, Western History Department/L. Mayard Dixon, p. 30; Grand Canyon National Park, photos # 15886 and # 4897, p. 31.

Diagrams and maps by Laura Westlund, pp. 8, 9, 12 13, 14, 22 © 1994 by Carolrhoda Books, Inc.

All rights reserved. International copyright secured. No part of this book may be reproduced, stored in a retrieval system, or transmitted in any form or by any means—electronic, mechanical, photocopying, recording, or otherwise—without the prior written permission of Carolrhoda Books, Inc., except for the inclusion of brief quotations in an acknowledged review.

First Avenue Editions
An imprint of Lerner Publishing Group
241 First Avenue North
Minneapolis, MN 55401 U.S.A.
Website address: www.lernerbooks.com

Library of Congress Cataloging-in-Publication Data

Cone, Patrick
    Grand Canyon / text and photographs by Patrick Cone.
        p.   cm. — (Nature in action)
    Includes index.
    ISBN 0-87614-628-0 (pbk. : alk. paper)
    1. Grand Canyon (Ariz.)—Juvenile literature. 1. Title. II. Series: Nature in action (Minneapolis, Minn.)
F788.C73 1994
979.1'32—dc20   93-31066

Manufactured in the United States of America
    7 8 9 10 11– JR – 08 07 06 05 04

Contents

For my father, Professor John H. Cone

In the Grand Canyon, rainbows arch from rim to rim after afternoon thunderstorms. Snow sparkles on tall spires where no human or other animal has set foot. Each sunrise and sunset paints the canyon with red light, and the rocks dazzle visitors with their colors: tan and red and black and orange.

The Grand Canyon is a deep crack in the earth cut by the Colorado River. Most of the canyon is at least a mile deep (deeper than a 500-story building is tall), and it can easily be seen from space. It wriggles like a snake across 280 miles of northwestern Arizona.

The river is over 100 feet deep in some places and about 300 feet wide. Dozens of small side canyons join the Colorado River like quills of a feather as the river flows from east to west through the canyon.

Over 18 miles wide in places, the Grand Canyon is less than 1 mile wide in others. Because of its enormous length, incredible depth, and the history that its rocks unveil, the canyon is one of the Natural Wonders of the World.

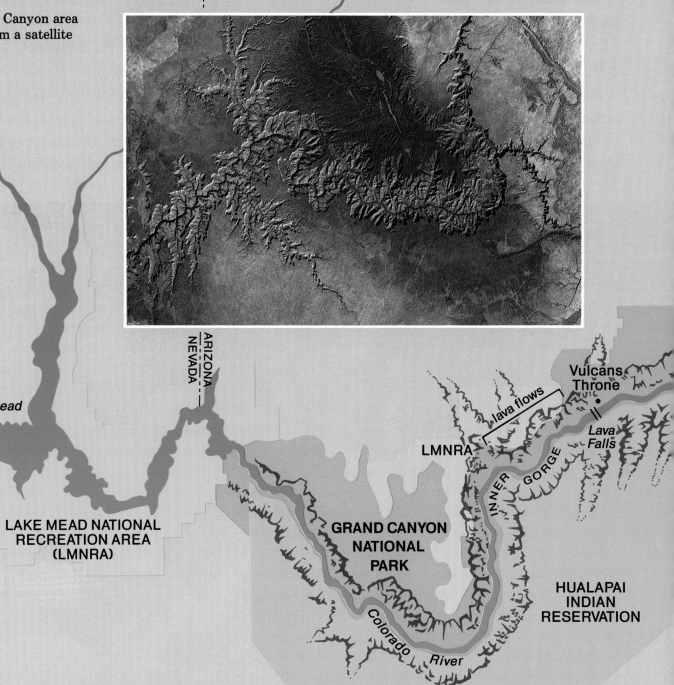

The Grand Canyon area
as seen from a satellite

N

Lake Mead

ARIZONA
NEVADA

HOOVER
DAM

ARIZONA
NEVADA

LAKE MEAD NATIONAL
RECREATION AREA
(LMNRA)

GRAND CANYON
NATIONAL
PARK

Colorado River

Vulcans
Throne

lava flows

LMNRA

INNER GORGE

Lava
Falls

HUALAPAI
INDIAN
RESERVATION

UTAH
ARIZONA

Lake Powell

GLEN
CANYON
DAM

Lees Ferry •

Kanab Creek

KAIBAB

NATIONAL

FOREST

KAIBAB
PLATEAU

MARBLE

CANYON

GRAND CANYON

NATIONAL

PARK

River

Colorado

• Supai

Crystal Creek

NORTH RIM

PAINTED DESERT

HAVASUPAI
INDIAN
RESERVATION

*Crystal
Rapids*

GRANITE

GORGE

SOUTH RIM

NAVAJO INDIAN
RESERVATION

KAIBAB

NATIONAL

FOREST

Little Colorado River

Miles

0   5   10   15

0   10   20

Kilometers

The story of the Grand Canyon is the story of Earth itself.
The canyon was shaped over
time by heat and cold, water
and wind. Oceans, rivers, earthquakes, volcanoes, and weather
have made the Grand Canyon
what it is today . . . and even now
continue to change it.

How Did the Canyon Rock Form?

Long before the Colorado River was even a trickling stream, the canyon's rocks were formed. Visitors who hike the canyon's trails, or shoot the river's rapids by raft, see almost two billion years of Earth's history in the stone walls. This amounts to half the planet's life!

The Grand Canyon is one of the best places in the world to study geology. All three of the basic types of rock are found there: sedimentary rock, metamorphic rock, and igneous rock.

Younger rocks lie on top of older ones, in all different colors and hardnesses. Each layer of rock in the canyon tells its own chapter of Earth's history. There are nearly two dozen distinct layers of rock in the canyon's walls, some thousands of feet thick. There are even layers missing. If we look closely, every layer of rock can tell us how and when it was made.

Oceans, Swamps, and Sand Dunes

Since the beginning of time, Earth's large sections of land, called continents, have been slowly drifting across the planet. In fact, Arizona used to be south of the equator until the land shifted slowly north. This movement of continents is called continental drift.

A shallow ocean once covered the Arizona land. On the bottom of the ocean, layers of seashells, dead plants, mud, and sand—called sediment—piled up.

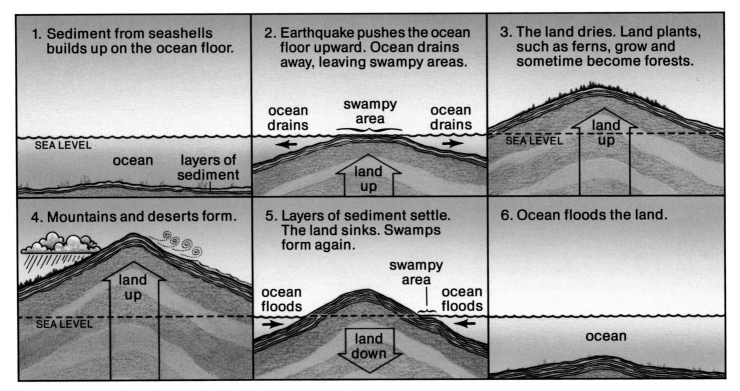

The cycle of changing landscape in the Grand Canyon area. At times it was too dry for forest plants to grow, and the land changed from forest to desert.

Hundreds of millions of years passed. The land was pushed upward by earthquakes, the ocean drained away, and the land gradually dried. The area changed from ocean to swamp to forest, and finally to desert.

As the land moved and then settled in, it sunk, and an ocean once again flooded the land. This change from ocean to desert to ocean to desert happened again and again for hundreds of millions of years.

More and more layers of new sediment sifted down and settled upon the older sediment. With the weight of the top sediment pressing down and the warmth of the earth heating them, the lower layers were pressed into solid rock. Rock made this way is called sedimentary rock.

Different kinds of sediment form different kinds of sedimentary rock. The countless tiny seashells from ocean animals turned into limestone. Mud from the ocean floor became shale. Sand dunes and beaches formed into sandstone. All of these distinct layers of sedimentary rock now rest on top of each other and can be seen in the colored ribbons of the canyon's cliffs.

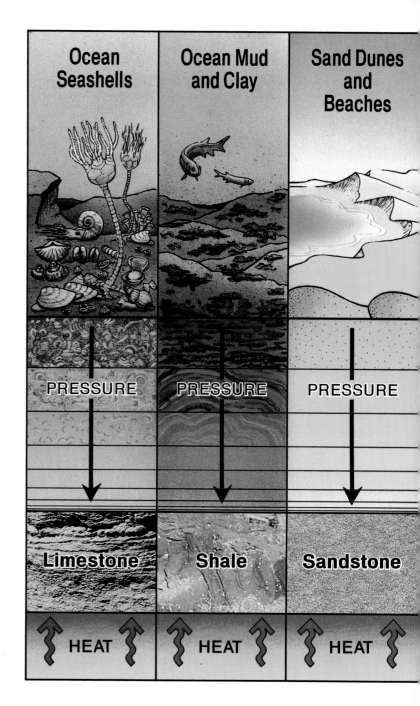

Rock Layers of the Grand Canyon

This diagram shows the layers of rock found in the walls of the main canyon next to the river. Many layers of rock above the 250-million-year-old layer have eroded.

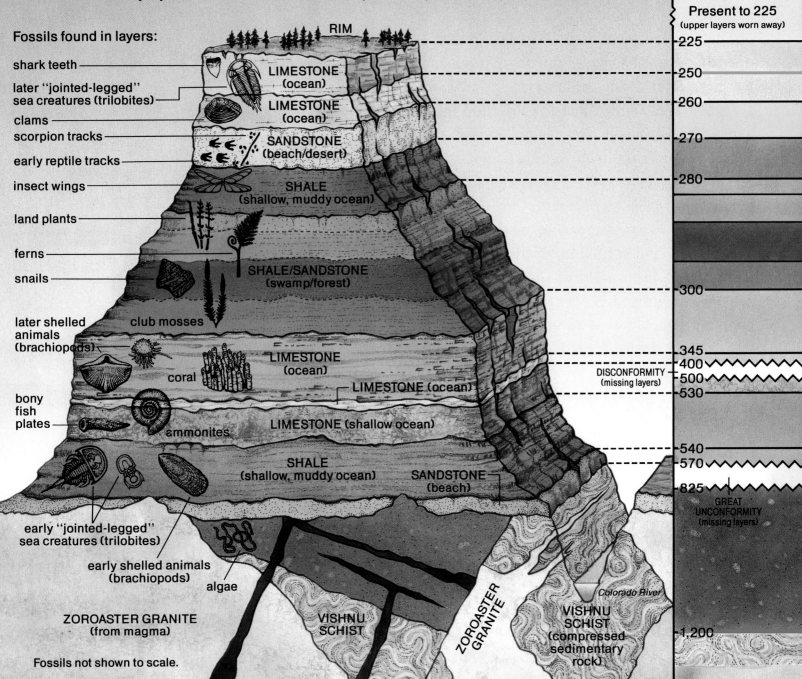

Fossils found in layers:

- shark teeth
- later "jointed-legged" sea creatures (trilobites)
- clams
- scorpion tracks
- early reptile tracks
- insect wings
- land plants
- ferns
- snails
- later shelled animals (brachiopods)
- club mosses
- coral
- bony fish plates
- ammonites
- early "jointed-legged" sea creatures (trilobites)
- early shelled animals (brachiopods)
- algae

RIM

LIMESTONE (ocean)

LIMESTONE (ocean)

SANDSTONE (beach/desert)

SHALE (shallow, muddy ocean)

SHALE/SANDSTONE (swamp/forest)

LIMESTONE (ocean)

LIMESTONE (ocean)

LIMESTONE (shallow ocean)

SHALE (shallow, muddy ocean)

SANDSTONE (beach)

ZOROASTER GRANITE (from magma)

VISHNU SCHIST

ZOROASTER GRANITE

VISHNU SCHIST (compressed sedimentary rock)

Colorado River

Fossils not shown to scale.

Approximate age (millions of years ago)

Present to 225 (upper layers worn away)

- 225
- 250
- 260
- 270
- 280
- 300
- 345
- 400
- 500 — DISCONFORMITY (missing layers)
- 530
- 540
- 570
- 825 — GREAT UNCONFORMITY (missing layers)
- 1,200

Wind, Rain, Snow, and Ice

The youngest, and therefore the highest, layer of rock in the Grand Canyon is a limestone that is over 250 million years old. This light brown sedimentary rock, like icing on a cake, tops the canyon walls. Younger layers, which would have been found above this limestone, have been worn away.

Rain, wind, snow, and ice wore away these layers of rock—like sandpaper wearing away wood—over a very long time. This process of wearing rock away is called erosion. Erosion is the force that carved the Grand Canyon.

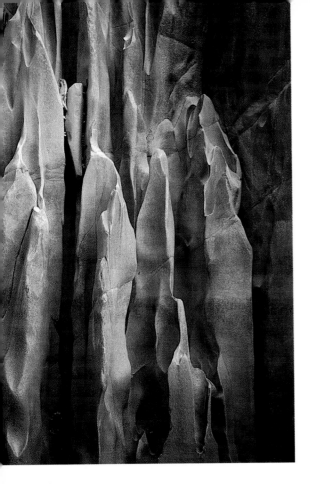

The softer the rock, the quicker it is worn away. As the wind, water, ice, and snow shave away at the canyon walls, holes form in the soft rock but not in the hard rock. This mixture of hard and soft rock has made the canyon's strangely shaped cliffs, mesas, and buttes.

16

Scientists can tell the age of each rock layer, but they were once puzzled by missing pieces in the canyon's history. There are gaps in the canyon's stone layers. Between two lower sedimentary layers, there was once another layer. But this rock eroded away before the next layer formed on top of it. Scientists call this 250-million-year gap of missing rock "The Great Unconformity." There are other missing layers, too. At one time, there had been additional layers on top of the canyon's rims, but these have also been worn away.

The Great Unconformity (below)

Vishnu schist (right); veins of Zoraster granite running through the Vishnu schist (right page)

Earth's Melting Pot

Underneath all the sedimentary rock layers lies the oldest rock in the canyon. Black and glossy, the Vishnu schist is over 1.5 billion years old, a third of the age of the earth. It is an example of metamorphic rock— rock that has changed from one kind of rock to another through heat and pressure.

The Vishnu schist began as the leftovers of ancient mountain ranges and sediment, buried deep underground. The weight and heat of the earth pressed and melted these bits of rock into a hard, glasslike rock. This black, glossy stone is found in the deepest part of the canyon, the Inner Gorge.

Earthquakes, Mountains, and Magma

While the canyon's rock layers were being formed, earthquakes shook the land. Some rock layers were buried by the shaking earth, and others were pushed upward to form mountains. In the Grand Canyon area, earthquakes thrust the land skyward.

The earthquakes also changed the rocks underneath the canyon. Thirty miles below ground is a hot, liquid rock called magma.

Thick and gooey like hot fudge, this molten rock pushed its way up into the cracks in the underground layers of the Vishnu schist. The magma cooled and formed pink and red veins of Zoroaster granite in the schist. Rock made from cooled magma, such as granite, is called igneous rock. Visitors can see the beautiful igneous rock laced through the black schist of the canyon's Inner Gorge.

How Did the Canyon Walls Form?

The Carving River

Nine million years ago, long after the last layer of canyon limestone had formed from ocean sediment, meandering streams flowed across the flat land. When the climate changed, the streams joined and grew in strength to become a mighty river. The river water carried sand, rock, and mud with it. These stones in the river were sent rushing over the sedimentary rock, cutting it like a saw. So while earthquakes were thrusting the land upward, the river was carving downward through the rock layers, and the Grand Canyon was born.

Over millions of years, the river grew, and so did the canyon. Today, the Colorado River is the largest river in the American Southwest. Its name comes from a Spanish word for "reddish colored," because of its muddy red water. The Colorado River starts high in the snow-covered Rocky Mountains and flows 1,450 miles before it empties into the Sea of Cortez near Baja, Mexico. As it flows, the river cuts the Grand Canyon deeper every single day, about seven inches every one thousand years.

Volcanoes and Lava Dams

While the river was slowly carving the canyon, other forces were at work. Throughout history, volcanoes have erupted in and near the canyon. From these fiery openings in the earth, the magma flowed up and above ground, becoming molten lava. The hot, black, bubbly lava cooled into a hard, igneous rock called basalt.

The basalt has dammed the canyon many times. Just one million years ago, lava poured from volcanoes into the river at Vulcans Throne in the Grand Canyon's western end. Steam and smoke filled the canyon, and a lake 150 miles long was created behind the lava dam. Slowly, the Colorado River cut through, and in some cases around, the hard basalt.

Close-up of lava flow, or basalt, in Vulcans Throne (left);
view from Lava Falls of eroded lava dams (above)

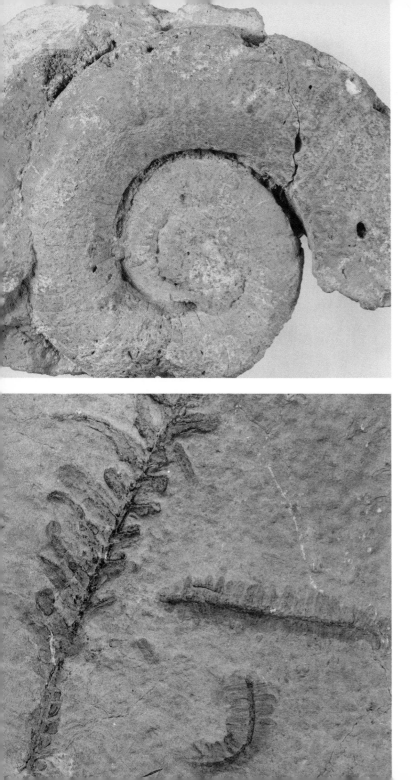

Fossils in limestone (lower left); shell fossil of an ammonite, an early sea animal (top left); drawing of a live ammonite (below)

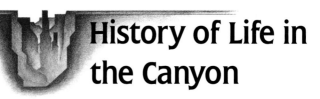

History of Life in the Canyon

Fossils and Early Life

The history of rocks, climate, and landscapes is not the only information recorded in the walls of the Grand Canyon. The history of life on Earth has also been frozen in the stone. Animals and plants that were buried in the sediment became part of the forming rock. The minerals in the plant and animal bodies were slowly replaced by minerals from the mud and water. The bodies turned to stones called fossils.

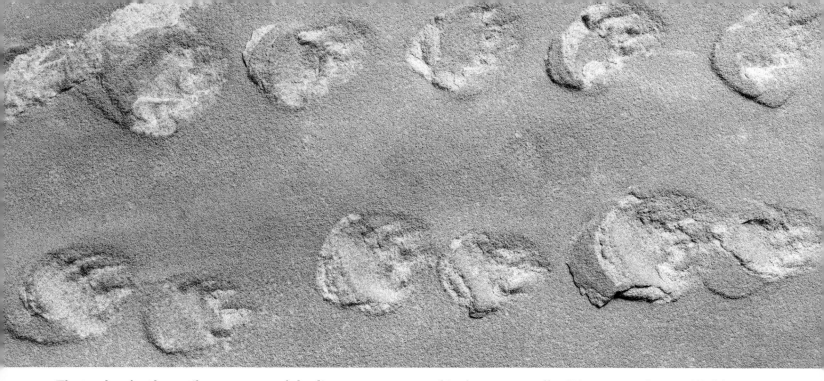

The tracks of early reptiles, ancestors of the dinosaurs, are trapped in the canyon walls. Dinosaur tracks, petrified forests, and fossils of early mammals are found throughout the canyons of the Southwest.

The oldest fossils ever found are of simple plants and one-celled animals. These have been discovered in the lower regions of the canyon walls.

In the middle limestone layers, fossils of 400-million-year-old fish, ferns, and insects have been uncovered.

Captured in the upper layers of sandstone are the fossilized tracks of dinosaurs from the Age of Reptiles—250 million years ago.

Finally, fossilized trees, called petrified wood, are all that remain of vast tropical forests that once covered the continent.

Only a few million years ago, saber-toothed tigers, enormous cave bears, mammoths, and giant sloths roamed the Grand Canyon. Vultures with 13-foot wingspans soared above the river. Miniature horses galloped across the grass plains near the cliffs. Now only skeletons and chips of bone remain of these amazing animals.

23

Humans are definitely the newcomers to the Grand Canyon.

Just as it took millions of years for each sedimentary layer of rock to form, grain by grain by grain, it took millions of years for plants and animals to develop. Compared to all this, human time is just a blink in history.

A beehive furnace used by early copper miners in the Grand Canyon to smelt ore (below); artifacts left by early European American miners and explorers (right)

If time could be speeded up, and one whole year could pass in one second, it would take 143 years to move from Earth's creation to the present. It would take about 47 of those years for all of the Grand Canyon's rock to form. And human history in this speeded-up time would take just two weeks!

Even so, the history of people in the Grand Canyon is rich and colorful.

Native Americans

About 9,000 to 3,000 years ago (7000 to 1000 B.C.), people traveled into the canyon area and stayed. With stone spears, they hunted deer, rabbits, and bighorn sheep. They roasted the fruit from prickly pear cactus, harvested beans from the native mesquite tree, and grew corn and squash along the riverbanks. Small deer statues of bent willow twigs and bits of their baskets and tools have been found in canyon caves. We call these early canyon dwellers the people of the Desert Culture.

For the time between 1000 B.C. and A.D. 500, scientists have found little proof that there were humans living in the Grand Canyon. No one is sure what happened to the people of the Desert Culture. They may have moved out of the area, looking for a place with more rain.

During the sixth century A.D., a new people, called the Hisatsinom, moved into the canyon area. They may have been distant relatives of the Desert Culture people. The Hisatsinom are also known as the Anasazi, which means "ancient ones" in Navajo.

The remains of a Hisatsinom (Anasazi) kiva

The Hisatsinom lived in the canyon from around A.D. 500 to A.D. 1140. They walked on trails and built footbridges of broken wood and branches. They made pottery, wove baskets, and stored their dried grain and beans in animal-proof stone shelters called granaries. Their homes were built with square stones, stacked without mortar. The buildings sometimes had round rooms known as kivas. These were used for religious ceremonies. Some of the kivas, homes, granaries, bridges, and trails of the Hisatsinom can still be seen.

25

Around A.D. 1140, a long drought forced the Hisatsinom out of the Grand Canyon to find food, but they did not go very far. Today's Hopi, Zuni, and Pueblo peoples are thought to be the descendants of the Hisatsinom.

The Hopi call themselves Hopituh, which means the "peaceful ones." They believe that their Hisatsinom ancestors passed through many worlds within the earth and then came up out of a small spring in the Grand Canyon. Hopi still gather at this salty blue spring on the Little Colorado River to collect salt for their religious ceremonies.

The sacred salt rock springs of the Hopi (above); the Hopi Corn Dance (right)

Paiute women going to the fields in the early 1900s

In addition to the Hopi, the Zuni, and the Pueblo peoples, the Pai nations settled in the canyonlands. Pai means "people." The Hualapai—"people of the pine trees"—live in the rugged southwestern end of the canyon, beyond Grand Canyon National Park.

The Havasupai—"people of the blue-green water"—make their home at the bottom of a southern side canyon. The town of Supai can be reached only by foot or mule.

The Paiutes—"water people" —settled on the northwest side of the Grand Canyon. Most Paiutes now live in Nevada and Utah.

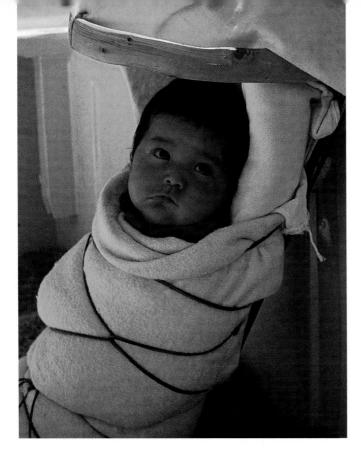

Between A.D. 1000 and 1400, the Navajo people migrated south from what is now Canada. The Navajo nation is the largest Native American nation in the United States, with over 200,000 people. Their huge reservation borders the southeast side of the Colorado River in the Grand Canyon, surrounding the tiny Hopi lands. Today many Navajo herd sheep on the sparse desert grasses and grow corn in the sandy soil.

Visiting the Grand Canyon area, you can see how present-day life mixes with the ancient. Over 1,200 sites with broken-down remains of early Native American stone buildings exist in the Grand Canyon area. Arrowheads and broken pottery can be found buried in the sand. Under overhanging cliffs and

boulders, ancient Native Americans once drew pictures of deer, bighorn sheep, the sun, rivers, and other mysterious objects. You can view the two types of rock drawings: pictographs and petroglyphs. Paintings on rock, often outlines of hands, are called pictographs. Petroglyphs are drawings carved into rock.

Over thousands of years, the dry desert air preserved many of these ancient objects. Left undisturbed, they will be able to teach us for years to come what it was like to live so long ago in the Grand Canyon.

European Americans

The first Europeans to see the Grand Canyon arrived in late September of 1540. A small group of Spanish soldiers led by Captain Garcia Lopez de Cardenas walked along the south edge of the Grand Canyon.

Two hundred and fifty years later, trappers, prospectors, ranchers, farmers, explorers, and adventurers were seeking their fortunes out west. America's first highways were its rivers, so some of these travelers tried to shoot down the violent Colorado River in boats. But it was too turbulent.

In 1869, Major John Wesley Powell led an expedition to map the Colorado River and the Grand Canyon. Funded by the Smithsonian Institution, the one-armed Powell and his men rowed three wooden boats all the way down the uncharted river. Powell named the enormous, many-colored canyon they entered, the Grand Canyon. Surviving their dangerous journey, they successfully mapped the unknown region.

When the soldiers of Cardenas first saw the canyon, they couldn't tell how big it was. Thinking the river was just a small stream, a few tried to hike down to it. But they gave up when they realized how big the canyon really was.

Early pioneers used Lees Ferry at the east end of the Grand Canyon to get across the river. Lees Ferry was one of the few places in the area where the Colorado River was not boxed in by high canyon walls and could be crossed safely. Now a bridge spans the Colorado River near Lees Ferry.

When stories of the canyon's mysterious and desolate beauty were told, the Grand Canyon soon became a popular tourist spot. Stagecoaches, steam trains, and automobiles filled with tourists rolled toward the canyon. Cablecars, bridges, roads, restaurants, tourist cabins, hotels, and campgrounds were built. Workers cut deep trails into the canyon for hikers, horses, and mule trains. More and more people came to visit the colored canyon.

The Grand Canyon Today

The National Park

Seeking to protect the canyon from damage by visitors, the U.S. government created Grand Canyon National Park in 1919. The park is larger than the state of Rhode Island, covering nearly 1,900 square miles. It lies between two man-made lakes, Lake Powell upstream and Lake Mead downstream.

The park protects all of the Colorado River banks between the lakes and about half of the many side canyons and their surrounding regions. Native American reservations, national forests, and wilderness areas cover the rest of the canyon's outer lands.

In the northeast, at Lees Ferry, water from Lake Powell enters Marble Canyon. Marble Canyon is a narrow, crooked canyon with sheer walls of polished limestone, which looks a little like marble. (Marble is a metamorphic rock, made from limestone.)

Marble Canyon is about 61 miles long, and the edges of its cliffs are just a few thousand feet above the river. Springs and waterfalls pour from cracks in the walls. Side canyons join Marble Canyon like doors in a hallway.

Water from a side canyon pours into Marble Canyon (left); Marble Canyon (below)

Where Marble Canyon ends, the Grand Canyon widens into a breathtaking vista. The Colorado River drops into the canyon's deep Inner Gorge of schist and granite. Here, earthquakes have pushed the cliff edges up. They rise twice as high above the river as they do in Marble Canyon.

Then for almost 200 miles, the Colorado River flows through the river wilderness, past side canyons, black cliffs, desert waterfalls, and Indian ruins. The river leaves the canyon at the gatelike Grand Wash Cliffs and flows into the low Nevada desert.

The Raging River

The Colorado River in the Grand Canyon runs swift and deep. It takes two full days for river water to travel the full length of the Grand Canyon. In those two days, the river drops over 2,000 feet in elevation.

Summer thunderstorms drop heavy rains that run off the bare rock into the narrow side canyons and sometimes cause flash floods. These fast-moving walls of water shoot down the streams in the side canyons toward the river, swallowing rocks, mud, and trees along the way. The water rushes into the Colorado River, where it drops its rock and mud, forming natural dams.

The river backs up in calm pools before spilling over the dams in rushing rapids. There are about 150 rapids in the Grand Canyon—one at every side canyon. The largest of these rapids drops over 40 feet. The longest rapid stretches for over a mile.

High above the raging Colorado River are the tops of the canyon walls. The two sides of the Grand Canyon are called the North and South Rims. These rims are high, flat table-lands. The eastern rims are part of the Kaibab Plateau. The Paiute word *Kaibab* means "mountain lying down." Like a steep set of stairs, cliffs of multicolored rock drop off from the plateaus of the North and South Rims to form the canyon below.

The elevation, or height above sea level, in the canyon varies from 9,165 feet on the North Rim to 7,000 feet on the South Rim. The highest points in the canyon are almost two miles above the lowest points. The river's elevation at the western end is only 1,200 feet.

Because of the high elevation, the air on the North Rim is thin, with less oxygen to breathe. The climate is subarctic, like that of central Canada. Summers are sunny, cool, and moist. The sun is harsh and quickly sunburns visitors. Winter snows smother the forests of ponderosa pine, spruce, and aspen trees on the Kaibab Plateau. Melting spring snows flow down through deep cracks in the rock and feed the canyon's many streams.

The South Rim, 2,000 feet lower than the North Rim, receives about half as much snow in its ponderosa pine forests. The climate is warmer and drier. Most visitors see the canyon for the first time from the South Rim.

As hikers walk down the trails on the canyon walls into the canyon, the temperature rises.

Those who walk from frigid snowbanks on the high rims to the searing, dry heat in the canyon's depths pass through many different climate zones along the way. For each 1,000 feet of elevation that people hike down into the canyon, the climate changes as if they had traveled 400 miles toward the equator. Down at the river, summer temperatures often soar above 100° F.

Animals and Plants

The different areas of elevation and climate have different animals and plants. On the rims, squirrels chatter in the tops of the tall timber. Flocks of wild turkeys wander the forest floor. Mountain lions hunt the mule deer that graze in the lush, grassy meadows. Coyotes chase down rabbits in the sagebrush valleys.

Just beneath the rims, desert bighorn sheep walk the canyon's narrow ledges to feed on dry grass. Ants, scorpions, tarantulas, and black widow spiders hide out in the cool, shadowy cracks. Hawks, eagles, ravens, and falcons—just 4 of the 200 known species of birds found in the canyon—ride the canyon's air currents.

A raven (above); desert bighorn sheep climb the canyon walls (right)

In the desert climate at the canyon bottom, still different types of plants and animals live. Barrel and cholla cactus store water in accordionlike trunks. The pink Grand Canyon rattlesnake, with its mildly poisonous bite, is shy and rarely seen.

Many of the animals survive the midday heat by sleeping during the day and coming out at night. King snakes, lizards, and gopher snakes hide from the sun and hunt during the cool nights. The long-tailed kangaroo rat also comes out at night. It never drinks liquids but makes water from the food it eats.

Sunset lights up the spikes of a cholla cactus; snowy egrets take off from the river (lower right); wildflowers bloom along the river (near top right); tamarisk trees (far top right)

Other plants and animals endure the desert heat in the canyon's bottom by living near water. Willow, mesquite, and tamarisk trees grow along streams and the riverbanks. Wildflowers, grass, and moss gather everywhere springs flow or water seeps.

Beaver, otters, and ringtail cats live near the river, along with egrets, herons, geese, and ducks. Golden eagles, their nests high on the sheer cliffs, fish for trout.

Twenty-one species of fish swim in the Colorado River and its streams. The rainbow trout, which were put into the river in Marble Canyon by scientists just thirty years ago, grow to record size. In the western end of the canyon, channel catfish, bass, and carp are more common.

On the top of the desert sand on the canyon floor is a brown crust that is a living being. Bacteria, fungi, and algae have bonded together in a crust in order to survive the harsh climate. Sometimes hundreds of years old, this cryptogamic soil keeps sand from blowing away in the wind. Cryptogamic means "hidden marriage."

Lichen is another marriage of fungi and algae, and it grows on bare rocks and tree trunks. Its patches of orange, brown, and green may be centuries old. Sometimes hikers accidentally kill the lichen and the living soil as they walk over them, not knowing what they are.

Dangers to the Canyon

More than four million people come to see the Grand Canyon every year. Many travel by car, bicycle, mule, and on foot. While most see the canyon from high on the rims, many others hike down into its depths on some of its hundreds of miles of trails.

Nearly 20,000 people see the Grand Canyon every year on exciting river-rafting trips. Some boats are powered only by oars and muscles, while large rafts have outboard motors. Airplanes and helicopters fly 350,000 people a year on tours, adding noise and pollution to the air, but leaving no footprints.

Every year, the number of visitors to the canyon goes up. More people means more traffic, more crowds, more litter, and even more crime. Buses and cars clog the narrow roads on busy days. Parking lots fill quickly, and campground sites must be reserved weeks ahead. Smoke from coal-burning power plants and copper smelters, and city smog often fill the once clear skies.

Upstream from the Grand Canyon, the Glen Canyon Dam controls the flow of the Colorado River to make electricity for Arizona's southern cities. Before the Glen Canyon Dam was built in the 1960s, the Colorado River ran freely through the Grand Canyon.

Every spring, muddy floods used to flow down the Colorado River from Wyoming and Utah. Canyon old-timers would say of the river, "It's too thick to drink, and too thin to plow." The muddy flood waters left behind sand, food, and minerals along the canyon's beaches. Plants and animals fed off this sediment.

Now the Glen Canyon Dam holds back some of the river, forming Lake Powell. Sometimes the dam lets out a little water and sometimes a lot. When the dam is opened wide, the water gushes down the Colorado River into the Grand Canyon. The rushing water has stranded boaters, eroded river beaches, and harmed the canyon's plants and animals.

Also, as the river water leaves the dam, the sand and mud are strained out. The humpback chub, a fish that has lived in the muddy waters of the Colorado and Little Colorado rivers for centuries, has been harmed by the cold, clear water. There are fewer chub than ever before. It is now an endangered species.

A scientist uses radio transmitters to study the endangered humpback chub fish.

Help on the Way

Despite the problems, people are working together to protect the Grand Canyon they love. Rangers, engineers, and scientists are busy studying the issues, trying to find ways to solve them.

For example, water from the Glen Canyon Dam is now let out more evenly. This has drastically cut down on the damage to the humpback chub and to beaches.

A nearby coal-burning power plant is being fitted with smokestack scrubbers to cut down the pollution in the sky over the canyon.

A steam locomotive has been built to bring tourists to the South Rim from near Flagstaff, Arizona, to lower the number of cars entering the park.

Patches earned by junior rangers (below)

River rafters and boaters are now required to take out everything they bring into the park with them, including garbage and human waste. River beaches are much cleaner than they were twenty years ago. Solar-powered outhouses have been set up on trails for hikers and backpackers.

Scientists are watching the canyon's plants and animals carefully to see how they live with so many humans near them. Anthropologists study the Native American ruins, pictographs, and petroglyphs, to see how to preserve them. National park rangers explain what these scientists have discovered to visitors to help them better understand the canyon.

Young visitors work in the park too. Kids in the Visitor Award Program become junior rangers. They study the plants, animals, geology, and weather, and pick up litter.

The Grand Canyon is a place of incredible mystery and beauty. It is both fragile and rugged, and it will be there long after we are all gone. By studying the Grand Canyon's past and present, we can try to learn what the future holds for the Grand Canyon, for us, and for our planet.

Fascinating Facts

New rapids form and old rapids are re-arranged every year. On December 8, 1966, the largest flash flood in 1,000 years roared down Crystal Creek, a side creek that meets the Colorado River in the middle of the Grand Canyon. In just a few moments, it created Crystal Rapids, one of the largest rapids in the Grand Canyon today.

Meteorites have helped shape the area around the Grand Canyon. In the 1920s, a meteorite slammed into a sandstone cliff above a Hualapai village in the western end of the canyon. There was no damage or loss of life, but the Hualapai quickly moved out of that part of the canyon.

Early Grand Canyon guide John Hance used to tell tourists that he had dug the Grand Canyon all by himself. On his deathbed, with his last breath, he turned to his close friends and whispered, "But where do you suppose I would have put all that dirt . . . ?"

When pioneers first saw the Grand Canyon, the area was judged as having little or no value. Cattle ranchers said of it, "It's a heck of a place to lose a cow."

During the early 1900s, mountain lions, coyotes, and wolves on the North Rim were hunted down and killed by settlers and forest rangers. Without these animals to hunt down weak and old mule deer, the deer herds soon grew too large for the food available.

Over the next decade, thousands of deer died of starvation as they competed for food. Today, rangers protect the mountain lions, coyotes, and other predators. The natural balance has returned, and both the predators and the deer herds are healthy.

Glossary

Basalt: A hard, black igneous rock formed from cooling lava

Butte: A high hill or ridge that rises steeply from a plain

Cholla: A spiny cactus with treelike limbs

Continent: One of the giant divisions of Earth's land

Continental drift: The slow, natural movement of giant divisions of land, called continents, across the surface of the earth

Cryptogamic soil: A brown, living crust of algae, fungi, and bacteria that protects loose sandy soil from wind

Earthquakes: The sudden shaking and breaking of the earth's crust

Erosion: The slow wearing away of rocks or soil by natural processes, such as rain, wind, ice, and snow

Fossils: The hardened remains of plants or animals preserved in rocks

Great Unconformity: The missing gap of one quarter of a billion years of rock near the bottom of the Grand Canyon walls

Igneous rock: Rock formed from magma, such as lava, granite, and basalt

Kaibab: Paiute word for the canyon's high plateaus that means "mountain lying down"

Lava: Magma that has flowed above ground

Lichen: A grouping of living algae and fungi

Limestone: Sedimentary rock formed from seashells

Magma: Molten rock deep in the earth

Marble: A hard, metamorphic rock made from sedimentary limestone

Mesa: Spanish word for flat-topped mountains

Metamorphic rock: Rock that has melted and changed form from the pressure of heat and weight, such as Vishnu schist and marble

Petrified wood: Wood that has turned to rock, or fossilized wood

Petroglyphs: Drawings carved into stone

Pictographs: Drawings painted on rock

Plateaus: Large, high, flat land areas

Rapids: Part of a river where water moves swiftly over rocks and other objects

Sediment: Bits of rock, sand, minerals, plants, and animals deposited by wind or water

Sedimentary rock: Rock formed from loose sediment pressed together, such as limestone, sandstone, and shale

Index